HOW WELL DO YOU KNOW THE HOLY BIBLE?

Bible Trivia

RAYFORD J. ELLIOTT

This book is a work of non-fiction. All scriptures were taken from the KJV, NIV, ESV, NKJV of the Holy Bible but are not noted.

CLF Publishing, LLC
www.clfpublishing.org
909.315.3161

ISBN# 978-1-9451023-7-0

Cover designed by Rayford J. Elliott

Printed in the United States of America

Dedication

This book is dedicated to all the Sunday school students who come every week with an open mind and heart to learn more of the Word of God. They diligently study every week and prepare to grab all they can from the teachings and discussions to strengthen their relationship with God. As a matter of fact, this is how the idea of writing a book containing trivia questions, brief commentary, and the supporting scriptures came about.

Every week, in addition to the study material we use, I text five trivia questions to the students. As a result, we have found it is a great tool to use to enhance their learning. I urge our Sunday school students at my church and all churches to continue to study to show yourselves approved. As II Timothy tells us in 2:15: *"Study to shew thyself approved unto God, a workman that needeth not to be ashamed, rightly dividing the word of truth."*

Preface

This book was written with the intent to help build one's relationship with God through learning more about Him through His Word. It is a book of trivia questions, comments, and scriptures to support the answers. It came out of the trivia questions I give my Sunday school students. Each week, I text them five trivia questions to help enhance their studies of the Word of God.

Sunday school is an important ministry in the church today, which is a means of educating believers. Sunday school started in the 1780's and was primarily for kids. This is no longer the case; it is now for adults as well as kids. Most churches today have sessions for children, young adults, and adults.

The basic foundation of the church is witnessing. That is what built the early church. The knowledge of God and your testimony together are powerful weapons for winning souls to God.

I hope you will find this book useful in increasing your knowledge and understanding through the trivia questions, explanations, and supported scriptures. *"And that from a child thou hast known the holy scriptures, which are able to make thee wise unto salvation through faith which is in Christ Jesus"* (II Timothy 3:15).

Introduction

There is only one book in the world that you can study all your life and continue to learn. With other books, you read them to learn their principles, and that is about the extent of it; they are no longer needed, and you go on to the next one. However, the Bible is non-exhaustive with the lessons it teaches. As you study and read it, there is always something else that will be revealed to you. It is the Book of Life; therefore, throughout your life, you will need it for your daily living. It provides you with principals and doctrines for living your life socially, politically, economically, psychologically, and above all spiritually. Thus, the question is, "Do you know the Bible?" There are many ways you can read it: vaingloriously, literally, and spiritually.

To read vaingloriously means it is read and studied to receive glory from others. Reading literally is to read and study to get the essence of it to use it as correctly as possible to adhere to what is being taught. Reading the Bible spiritually is the best way to read. When you read it spiritually, you read it with expectancy. You know it has answers for your daily living. The spiritual will supersede all other methods. It has all the answers through justification, sanctification, and salvation. We all need to be justified, sanctified and saved by our Lord and Savior Jesus Christ. The Bible tells us how that can be done.

Like many things in life, the more knowledge and understanding you have, the better you can cling to what the Bible is telling you. So, do you know the Bible?

Unlike any other book, the Bible is not just a book of knowledge; rather, it is also a book of relationship. Thus, we all can build and strengthen our relationship with God. Like any relationship, the more you associate and communicate with God's Word, the stronger the relationship. This relationship manifests itself with the Word of God, which is the Bible.

This book is designed to help you build your relationship with God. It is done by using trivia questions, which will capture your interest and curiosity by the use of various Biblical facts and stories. Good questions have a tendency to attract and create a sense of wonder and curiosity. That is what this book will create in you, so that your relationship with God grows stronger, as you receive the amazing Word of God.

This book is limited in the number of questions that it contains. After all, there are literally thousands of questions that can be asked. As such, I speculate there will be a series of books in this format to come in the near future.

May the grace of God continue to be with you, and may His blessings continue to rain down on you.

God bless!!

Who was the first to be called a prophet in the Bible?

A prophet is a special chosen one by God to carry out His will. He prays for others and foresees things other believers cannot see. After his wife Sarah was returned to him via God's command, Abraham prayed for Abimelek (who had Abraham's wife), so he would live. Abraham was the first to be called a prophet.

✝ ✝ ✝ ✝ ✝ ✝ ✝ ✝

"Then God said to him in the dream, 'Yes, I know you did this with a clear conscience, and so I have kept you from sinning against me. That is why I did not let you touch her. Now return the man's wife, for he is a prophet, and he will pray for you and you will live'" (Genesis 20: 6-7).

Who does the Bible record as having the first dream?

Dreams are one of the ways God speaks to people. God spoke to Abimelek concerning Sarah, Abraham's wife. God's words to him were to return Abraham's wife back to him. He was recorded as the first person God spoke to through a dream. However, it should be noted that Abimelech was not a believer. That shows the power of God and how He will use whatever means in His will to accomplish what His will may be.

✝ ✝ ✝ ✝ ✝ ✝ ✝ ✝

"But God came to Abimelek in a dream one night and said to him, 'You are as good as dead because of the woman you have taken; she is a married woman'" (Genesis 20:3).

How was Moses different from other prophets in the Bible?

The elects of God are chosen at His discretion. What God put together no man can set it apart. God chooses to communicate to His elect as His godly authority allows. He communicates with some through dreams, visions, or other people, to name a few. Moses was unique in that God chose to speak to him face-to-face like no other prophet.

"Then He said, 'Hear now My words: If there is a prophet among you, I, the LORD, make Myself known to him in a vision; I speak to him in a dream.' Not so with My servant Moses; He is faithful in all My house. I speak with him face to face, Even plainly, and not in dark sayings; And he sees the form of the LORD. Why then were you not afraid To speak against My servant Moses?'" (Numbers 12:6-8).

Who were the first persons an angel spoke to in the OT and NT?

Another unique way God speaks to us is through His angels. Several times an angel spoke to a person in the Old and New Testaments. Note- these two persons were women: Hagar and Mary.

✝ ✝ ✝ ✝ ✝ ✝ ✝ ✝

"Then the angel of God called to Hagar out of heaven, and said to her, "What ails you, Hagar? Fear not, for God has heard the voice of the lad where he is" (Genesis 21:17).

"Then the angel said to her, "Do not be afraid, Mary, for you have found favor with God" (Luke 1:30).

Which are the longest and shortest chapters in the Bible?

The Bible that the majority of churches and believers use is the Bible that has 66 books. There are 39 books in the Old Testament and 27 in the New Testament. However, other religious secs have different number of books in their Bible. For example, the Catholic Bible has 73 books, the Protestant Bible has 80 books, and the Ethiopian Orthodox Bible has 81 books.

Most denominations use the 66 book Bible. In this Bible, the shortest chapter is Psalm 117, which has only two verses and twenty-nine words. The longest chapter of the Bible is Psalm 119, which has 176 verses.

What did God send to protect Daniel in the lions' den?

Daniel was a prophet and a strong believer in God and His Word. He refused to honor a pagan custom mandated by the pagan king. He was thrown into a lion's den to be eaten by the lions because of his refusal to obey the king's mandate. As a servant of God, God protected Daniel in the lions' den by sending an angel to shut the mouth of the lions.

Angels are a part of the saints' lives today. They are looking over us and ministering to us.

✝ ✝ ✝ ✝ ✝ ✝ ✝ ✝

"My God sent His angel and shut the lions' mouths, so that they have not hurt me, because I was found innocent before Him; and also, O king, I have done no wrong before you" (Daniel 6:22).

What did God send to feed Elijah while he was hiding in the Brook (ravine) near the Jordan river?

After Elijah told Ahab there would be a famine for three years in the land, he fled to the ravine because he feared for his life at the hand of the king. He found himself in a desolate place where there was no food to live. God sent the ravens to supply him with meat and bread. God will supply all of our needs according to His riches and glory. We don't have to worry about tomorrow. God has it covered.

✝ ✝ ✝ ✝ ✝ ✝ ✝ ✝

"So he went and did according to the word of the LORD, for he went and stayed by the Brook Cherith, which flows into the Jordan. The ravens brought him bread and meat in the morning, and bread and meat in the evening; and he drank from the brook" (I Kings 17:5-6).

Who was the first to prophesy in the Bible?

The Bible is full of prophets. A prophet is a God chosen person who delivers messages from God. The book of Jude says Enoch was "the seventh from Adam." He prophesied about the judgement to come on man.

✝ ✝ ✝ ✝ ✝ ✝ ✝ ✝

"Now Enoch, the seventh from Adam, prophesied about these men also, saying, 'Behold, the Lord comes with ten thousand of His saints, to execute judgment on all, to convict all who are ungodly among them of all their ungodly deeds which they have committed in an ungodly way, and of all the harsh things which ungodly sinners have spoken against Him'" (Jude 14).

Who had the first recorded vision in the Bible?

God speaks to His people in many ways: dreams, visions, other people, and circumstances. However, it is important to have a discernment to know God is speaking to you and not some other entity.

The first recorded vision is when God is communicating with Abraham. This occurred when God made a covenant with Abraham. Abraham was childless at the time, and God wanted to assure him the he and his offspring are the chosen ones.

✝ ✝ ✝ ✝ ✝ ✝ ✝ ✝

"After these things the word of the LORD came to Abram in a vision, saying, 'Do not be afraid, Abram. I am your shield, your exceedingly great reward'" (Genesis 15:1).

Who made the first clothes for Adam and Eve?

When Adam and Eve sinned, they realized they were naked and proceeded to hide themselves with leaves. When God came and saw what they had done, judgement was placed on them. After He declared judgement on the serpent, God decided to properly dress Adam and Eve. Instead of the leaves, He made clothes for them from animal skin.

"Also for Adam and his wife the LORD God made tunics of skin, and clothed them" (Genesis 3:21).

How many people could have saved Sodom and Gomorrah?

When Abraham was visited by the three strangers, including the Lord Jesus, he interceded for Sodom and Gomorrah because he did not want the righteous to be destroyed with the wicked. The Lord said he will spare the cities if there were 50 righteous in the city. There were none. Then 45 was suggested, then 30, 20 and 10. There were none found righteous in the cities. These cities were plagued with sin, and there was no turning back on the judgment that was brought upon them because of their sin. Ten could not be found righteous to save the cities.

✝ ✝ ✝ ✝ ✝ ✝ ✝ ✝

"Then he said, 'Let not the Lord be angry, and I will speak but once more: Suppose ten should be found there?' And He said, 'I will not destroy it for the sake of ten'" (Genesis 18:32).

Who was taken to heaven alive?

As Elisha was walking along with his mentor and teacher Elijah, he asked for a double portion of Elijah's spirit. Then, a chariot of fire came and separated them and a whirlwind came and took Elijah up into heaven.

Enoch was the great grandfather of Noah. He was a strong believer in God, walked in righteousness, and served God. Enoch walked with God, and God took him.

$$\maltese \quad \maltese \quad \maltese \quad \maltese \quad \maltese \quad \maltese \quad \maltese \quad \maltese$$

"So he said, "You have asked a hard thing. Nevertheless, *if you see me when I am taken from you, it shall be so for you; but if not, it shall not be so." Then it happened, as they continued on and talked, that suddenly a chariot of fire* appeared *with horses of fire, and separated the two of them; and Elijah went up by a whirlwind into heaven"* (II Kings 2:10-11).

"So all the days of Enoch were three hundred and sixty-five years. And Enoch walked with God; and he was not, for God took him" (Genesis 5:23-24).

Who was the first person to raise someone from the dead?

Elijah, the prophet, met a woman with a son. This woman made bread for Elijah to eat when she had only enough flour to feed herself and her son. But she recognized him as a man of God. Later, her son died, and Elijah came, breathed on him, and brought him back to life.

✝ ✝ ✝ ✝ ✝ ✝ ✝ ✝

"'Give me your son,' Elijah replied. He took him from her arms, carried him to the upper room where he was staying, and laid him on his bed. Then he cried out to the LORD, 'LORD my God, have you brought tragedy even on this widow I am staying with, by causing her son to die?' Then he stretched himself out on the boy three times and cried out to the LORD, 'LORD my God, let this boy's life return to him!' The LORD heard Elijah's cry, and the boy's life returned to him, and he lived" (I Kings 17:19-23).

How did Paul's friends help him escape from Damascus?

After Paul's (then called Saul) blindness was healed, after the divine experience on the road to Damascus, he began to preach the Gospel of Jesus Christ in the synagogues in Damascus. The people did not really accept him because they had heard of what he was and what his original objective was. They then began to plot to kill him in this city. They watched him and waited for the opportune time to kill him. But, his friends lowered him down in a basket one night where he was preaching to help him escape from the city. He then went to Jerusalem to preach.

✝ ✝ ✝ ✝ ✝ ✝ ✝ ✝

"After many days had gone by, there was a conspiracy among the Jews to kill him, but Saul learned of their plan. Day and night, they kept close watch on the city gates in order to kill him. But his followers took him by night and lowered him in a basket through an opening in the wall" (Acts 9:23-25).

What type of wood did Noah use to make the ark?

Noah was a righteous man, blameless among the people of his time, and walked faithfully with God. The earth was corrupt in God's sight and was full of wickedness. God brought judgement to the earth and concluded He would put an end to all people. Because Noah was the only one found to be righteous and faithful to God, God spared him and his family. God told Noah water will be the source of man's destruction on earth and for him to make an ark made of cypress wood.

✝ ✝ ✝ ✝ ✝ ✝ ✝ ✝

"God saw how corrupt the earth had become, for all the people on earth had corrupted their ways. So God said to Noah, 'I am going to put an end to all people, for the earth is filled with violence because of them. I am surely going to destroy both them and the earth. So make yourself an ark of cypress wood; make rooms in it and coat it with pitch inside and out'" (Genesis 6:12-14).

How high did the water rise during the flooding?

For forty days, it rained continually. The water began to rise, and the ark was lifted with all the appointed and designated people and animals, which God had selected to survive. All the mountains on the whole earth ended up being covered with water. The water rose above the highest mountain 15 cubits (22 feet and six inches).

✝ ✝ ✝ ✝ ✝ ✝ ✝ ✝

"For forty days the flood kept coming on the earth, and as the waters increased, they lifted the ark high above the earth. The waters rose and increased greatly on the earth, and the ark floated on the surface of the water. They rose greatly on the earth, and all the high mountains under the entire heavens were covered. The waters rose and covered the mountains to a depth of more than fifteen cubits" (Genesis 7:17-20).

What creature did Moses run away from?

After Moses had his encounter with the burning bush on Mount Horeb, God told him to go to the king of Egypt and take God's message concerning His people. Moses began to doubt whether the people would listen to him. God made it clear He would not let Moses go on an assignment without being prepared. He asked Moses what was in his hand. Moses said a staff. God told him to throw it down; it immediately became a snake, and Moses ran from it. God called him back and told him to pick it up, and it turned back into his staff.

"Then the LORD said to him, 'What is that in your hand?' 'A staff,' he replied. The LORD said, 'Throw it on the ground.' Moses threw it on the ground and it became a snake, and he ran from it. Then the LORD said to him, 'Reach out your hand and take it by the tail.' So Moses reached out and took hold of the snake and it turned back into a staff in his hand" (Exodus 4:2-4).

When was man given permission to eat meat?

After the flood, when Noah was on dry land, he built an altar unto the Lord. He also offered a burnt offering unto Him. The Lord saw this and said He will never again curse the ground again.

Before the flood, man only ate plants and vegetables; he was primarily a vegetarian. During the flood, all vegetation and plants were consumed by the water. It was then that God told man he can eat meat. However, there were certain kinds of animals he was to refrain from eating.

✝ ✝ ✝ ✝ ✝ ✝ ✝ ✝

"The fear and dread of you will fall on all the beasts of the earth, and on all the birds in the sky, on every creature that moves along the ground, and on all the fish in the sea; they are given into your hands. Everything that lives and moves about will be food for you. Just as I gave you the green plants, I now give you everything. But you must not eat meat that has its lifeblood still in it" (Genesis 9:2-4).

What was in the Ark of the Covenant?

The Ark of the Covenant is a gold-covered wooden chest with a lid that carried three of the most precious objects possessed by the Israelites. One was the two tablets the Ten Commandments were written on and some of the manna the Israelites were given by God to eat on their way to the Promise Land. And the other object was the staff of Aaron.

"Behind the second curtain was a room called the Most Holy Place, which had the golden altar of incense and the gold-covered ark of the covenant. This ark contained the gold jar of manna, Aaron's staff that had budded, and the stone tablets of the covenant" (Hebrews 9:3-4).

How many men did it take to carry a cluster of grapes the spies found in the Promise Land?

The Lord told Moses to send out some men to explore the land of Canaan. Moses selected twelve men that represented each one of the tribes. They were the leaders of the tribes. They explored the land for a period of forty days. At one location, they found grapes that were big and full. The spies wanted to carry some of the grapes back to camp to show Moses and the people how rich and fertile the land was. It took two men to carry one cluster of grapes.

✝ ✝ ✝ ✝ ✝ ✝ ✝ ✝

"So they went up and explored the land from the Desert of Zin as far as Rehob, toward Lebo Hamath. They went up through the Negev and came to Hebron, where Ahiman, Sheshai and Talmai, the descendants of Anak, lived. (Hebron had been built seven years before Zoan in Egypt.) When they reached the Valley of Eshkol, they cut off a branch bearing a single cluster of grapes. Two of them carried it on a pole between them, along with some pomegranates and figs" (Numbers 1:21-23).

How long was the ark afloat before the water abated?

During the time of the flood, it rained for forty days and nights. The water covered the whole earth. Noah was 600 years old when the rain came. Noah was 601 years and ten days old before he saw the ground again. The ark was afloat for a total of one hundred fifty days.

✝ ✝ ✝ ✝ ✝ ✝ ✝ ✝

"But God remembered Noah and all the wild animals and the livestock that were with him in the ark, and he sent a wind over the earth, and the waters receded. Now the springs of the deep and the floodgates of the heavens had been closed, and the rain had stopped falling from the sky. The water receded steadily from the earth. At the end of the hundred and fifty days the water had gone down, and on the seventeenth day of the seventh month the ark came to rest on the mountains of Ararat" (Genesis 8:1-4).

How many braids of hair did Sampson have?

Sampson was a Nazarite, a person who is set aside by God to carry out a certain mission. Sampson was given a specific ability by God to use while leading God's people back to Him. God gave him physical strength, which was manifested in his hair. Before Sampson was born, God told his mother never to cut his hair and that he was to refrain from drinking wine. Sampson wore his long hair braided. There were seven braids.

✟ ✟ ✟ ✟ ✟ ✟ ✟ ✟

"Delilah realized he had told her everything. So she sent a message to the Philistine rulers. She said, 'Come back one more time. He has told me everything.' So the rulers returned. They brought the silver with them. Delilah got Samson to go to sleep on her lap. Then she called for someone to shave off the seven braids of his hair. That's how she began to bring Samson under her control. And he wasn't strong anymore" (Judges 16:18-10).

Who was once saved from death by a talking donkey?

Balaam was a man whom God spoke to, telling him not to go with the Moabs to curse the people of Israel. He disobeyed and saddled his donkey the next morning to go with them. As he traveled, an angel stood in the middle of the road to stop him. His mind and heart were not open to see the angel. The donkey saw the danger and went off the road to the vineyard to save Balaam from the danger ahead. When Balaam chastised the donkey, God put words in the donkey's mouth to speak to Balaam.

"And when the ass saw the angel of the LORD, she fell down under Balaam: and Balaam's anger was kindled, and he smote the ass with a staff. And the LORD opened the mouth of the ass, and she said unto Balaam, What have I done unto thee, that thou hast smitten me these three times? And Balaam said unto the ass, Because thou hast mocked me: I would there were a sword in mine hand, for now would I kill thee. And the ass said unto Balaam, Am not I thine ass, upon which thou hast ridden ever since I was thine unto this day? was I ever wont to do so unto thee? and he said, Nay" (Numbers 22:21-33).

How many Proverbs and Psalms did Solomon write?

A proverb is literally a short saying that gives advice about how people should live or that expresses a belief that is generally thought to be true. Proverbs are a part of the poetical books in the Bible. Biblical proverbs offer advice regarding many aspects of life. They are not prophecies, but guidelines on how to live a victorious, fulfilled life. They give vivid details displaying romance or a dialog between two people.

The psalms are one of the most quoted and used scripture in the Bible because they offer encouragement and judgement that can be brought upon people. They point the way to blessings and warnings of divine judgement.

Solomon is known as a writer of proverbs and psalms. He wrote three thousand proverbs and one thousand and five psalms.

Who became queen by winning a beauty contest?

When King Xerxes no longer wanted Queen Vashti as queen because of her disobedience to him, he put out a call for thousands of women to be brought to him, so he could choose a replacement for Queen Vashti. But, there were certain criteria they were required to meet. Two of the requirements were they had to be a virgin and beautiful. Esther, who was a Jewish woman, became one of the contestants. The king viewed many women but was not successful in finding one that suited his desires- until Esther appeared. He chose her to be the next queen. It was not due to her skills, education, family ties, or profession; it was her beauty.

"Then said the king's servants that ministered unto him, Let there be beautiful young virgins sought out for the king" (Esther 2:2).

"And the king loved Esther more than all the women, and she obtained grace and favor in his sight more than all the virgins; so that he set the royal crown upon her head, and made her queen instead of Vashti" (Esther 2:17).

Who wanted to pay Peter and John for the power to give people the Holy Spirit?

Just before Jesus left the earth, He said He would not leave us helpless and that He would send us a helper, a comforter to help us through our life. This helper is available for everyone, and all we have to do to receive Him is to accept Jesus Christ as our savior, believe He died and was raised from the grave. This helper is none other than the Holy Spirit. However, the Holy Spirit cannot be bought or sold. Jesus gave the power to the apostles to lead the unsaved to the Holy Spirit by the laying on of hands. There was a man name Simon who witnessed an experience Peter and John were involved in, and he desired the power to give the Holy Spirit to others, and he was willing to pay money.

✝ ✝ ✝ ✝ ✝ ✝ ✝ ✝

"And when Simon saw that through laying on of the apostles' hands the Holy Ghost was given, he offered them money, Saying, give me also this power, that on whomsoever I lay hands, he may receive the Holy Ghost" (Acts 8:18-19).

Why did Job sacrifice a burnt offering every morning?

One of the most faithful believers in the Bible is Job. Job was a God-fearing man and had dedicated his life to following God's commands. God recognized that about him and trusted him in doing His will. As a result, God allowed him to be tested by Satan himself, to show the unmovable faith Job had in God. In service to God, Job would offer a bunt offering every morning in an effort to atone sin. He did this regularly in case one of his children had sinned.

✝ ✝ ✝ ✝ ✝ ✝ ✝ ✝

"And it was so, when the days of their feasting were gone about, that Job sent and sanctified them, and rose up early in the morning, and offered burnt offerings according to the number of them all: for Job said, It may be that my sons have sinned, and cursed God in their hearts. Thus did Job continually" (Job 1:5).

How did Jesus heal the mute man?

Jesus had just returned from a trip across the sea of Galilee. On the shore, a group of men were carrying a man who was deaf and could not speak. The men asked Jesus to lay His hands on him. Evidently, they had heard about Jesus and had faith in who Jesus is. Jesus took the man aside and stuck His finger in His ear. Then, He spat and touched the man's tongue.

✝ ✝ ✝ ✝ ✝ ✝ ✝ ✝

"And they bring unto him one that was deaf, and had an impediment in his speech; and they beseech him to put his hand upon him. And he took him aside from the multitude, and put his fingers into his ears, and he spit, and touched his tongue; And looking up to heaven, he sighed, and saith unto him, Ephphatha, that is, Be opened. And straightway his ears were opened, and the string of his tongue was loosed, and he spake plain" (Luke 7:32-35).

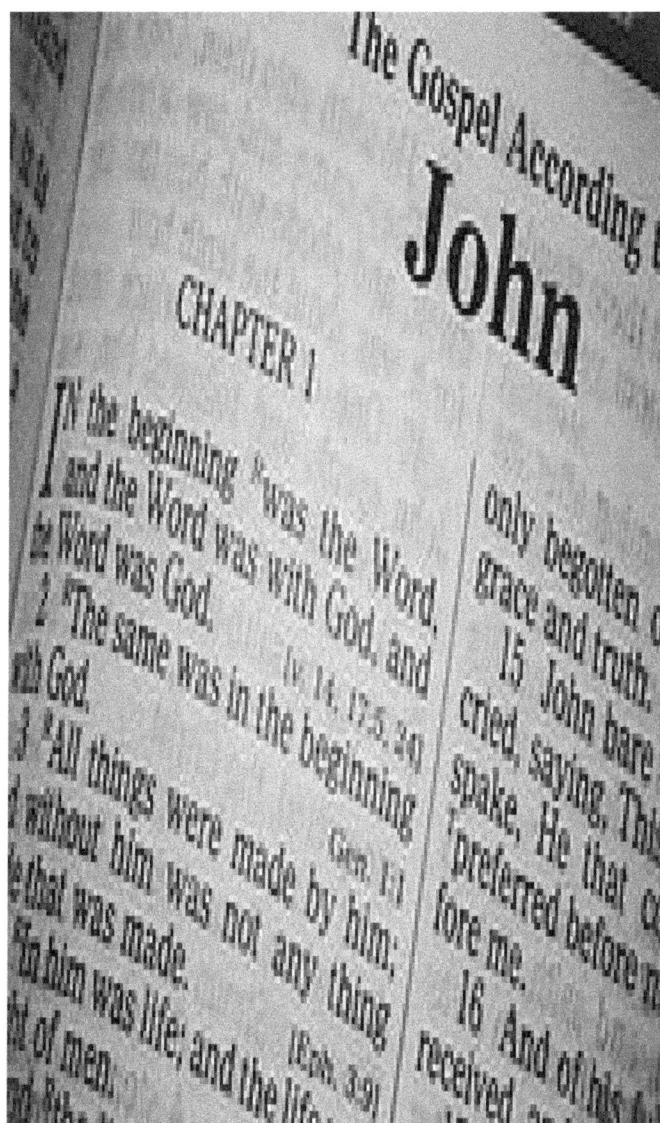

What happened to Nebuchadnezzar when he went insane?

Nebuchadnezzar was king, and he became consumed by what he had, causing pride to infiltrate his heart. He did not recognize the glory of God or His work. He became very boastful in all of his accomplishments. God decided to take his kingdom away from him, and he was stricken by insanity. During his insanity, he grew claws like a bird, feathers like an eagle, and ate grass like a cow.

✝ ✝ ✚ ✚ ✝ ✝ ✠ ✦

"The same hour was the thing fulfilled upon Nebuchadnezzar: and he was driven from men, and did eat grass as oxen, and his body was wet with the dew of heaven, till his hairs were grown like eagles' feathers, and his nails like birds' claws" (Daniel 4:33).

How many times did King David say, "I have sinned"?

David is one of the most popular characters in the Bible. He is known as the man after God's own heart. He was a strong believer in God and worked hard to adhere to God's commands. However, like so many men, he erred. He did things that were out of line with the Word of God. In other words, he sinned. Some of his sins resulted in great consequences. On the other hand, he praised and worshiped God. One unique trait about him is when he sinned, he knew how to seek God and ask for forgiveness. Six times he spoke the words, "I have sinned." In I Chronicles, he said, "I have sinned greatly."

✝ ✝ ✝ ✝ ✝ ✝ ✝ ✝

"And David said unto Nathan, I have sinned against the LORD" (II Samuel 12:13).

"And David's heart smote him after that he had numbered the people. And David said unto the LORD, I have sinned" (II Samuel 24:10).

"And David spake unto the LORD when he saw the angel that smote the people, and said, Lo, I have sinned" (II Samuel 24:17).
"I said, LORD, be merciful unto me: heal my soul; for I have sinned against thee" (Psalm 41:4).

"Against thee, thee only, have I sinned" (Psalm 51:4).

"And David said unto God, I have sinned greatly" (I Chronicles 21:8).

Which prophet caused the iron ax to float in water?

The men that accompanied Elijah as he traveled to the Jordan river stopped and began to chop wood to use to setup camp. While one man was chopping the wood, the ax head fell into the river. They told Elijah what happened and that they couldn't chop the wood without the ax head. Elijah took a stick and threw it in the river where the ax head had fallen. The ax came from the bottom of the river and floated on the water.

"They went to the Jordan and began to cut down trees. As one of them was cutting down a tree, the iron ax head fell into the water. 'Oh no, my lord!' he cried out. 'It was borrowed!'" (II Kings 6:5).

"The man of God asked, 'Where did it fall?' When he showed him the place, Elisha cut a stick and threw it there, and made the iron float. 'Lift it out,' he said. Then the man reached out his hand and took it" (II Kings 6:6).

After Joshua's army took over Canaan, what did they do to their enemy's horses?

Joshua and his army defeated the Canaanites through battle and chased them out of the land. There were about ten thousand of the enemy's horses remaining in the land. Joshua had all of the horses' hamstrings cut, so they could not be used in case they fell into the hands of the enemy again. He also burned all of their chariots.

✝ ✝ ✝ ✝ ✝ ✝ ✝ ✝

"So Joshua and his whole army came against them suddenly at the Waters of Merom and attacked them, and the LORD gave them into the hand of Israel. They defeated them and pursued them all the way to Greater Sidon, to Misrephoth Maim, and to the Valley of Mizpah on the east, until no survivors were left. Joshua did to them as the LORD had directed: He hamstrung their horses and burned their chariots" (Joshua 11:7-9).

Who was the first person recorded to have worn a veil?

Before Isaac married Rebekah, he met her on his return trip from Beer Lahai Roi. He was out in the field praying when Rebekah was passing by. She looked and asked her servant who he was. The servant said Isaac was his master. She then immediately took her veil and covered herself out of respect and custom.

✝ ✝ ✝ ✝ ✝ ✝ ✝ ✝

"Now Isaac had come from Beer Lahai Roi, for he was living in the Negev. He went out to the field one evening to meditate, and as he looked up, he saw camels approaching. Rebekah also looked up and saw Isaac. She got down from her camel and asked the servant, 'Who is that man in the field coming to meet us?' 'He is my master,' the servant answered. So she took her veil and covered herself" (Genesis 24:64-65).

Who was the only man in the Bible described as short?

When Jesus went to Jericho, there was a man called Zacchaeus who wanted to see Him. Zacchaeus was a rich man. Because he was too short to see over the crowd, he climbed up a sycamore tree. Jesus saw him in the tree as he was passing by and told him to come down because he wanted to stay at his house.

✝ ✝ ✝ ✝ ✝ ✝ ✝ ✝

"Jesus entered Jericho and was passing through. A man was there by the name of Zacchaeus; he was a chief tax collector and was wealthy. He wanted to see who Jesus was, but because he was short he could not see over the crowd. So he ran ahead and climbed a sycamore tree to see him, since Jesus was coming that way. When Jesus reached the spot, he looked up and said to him, 'Zacchaeus, come down immediately. I must stay at your house today.' So he came down at once and welcomed him gladly" (Luke 19:1-3).

Who was designated to carry the Ark of the Covenant?

The Ark of the Covenant was a sacred chest made by the Israelites according to the command and design of God. It held in it the tablets the Ten Commandments were written on, Aaron's staff, and manna (the food God had supplied the Israelites while they were traveling to the Promise Land). Only the Levites could carry the Ark.

"After David had constructed buildings for himself in the City of David, he prepared a place for the ark of God and pitched a tent for it. Then David said, 'No one but the Levites may carry the ark of God, because the LORD chose them to carry the ark of the LORD and to minister before him forever'" (I Chronicles 15:1-2).

Which prophet prophesied the coming of John the Baptist?

John the Baptist is known as the forerunner of Jesus Christ. In other words, he was the one God planned to come before Jesus. His assignment was to introduce Jesus to the world as the Messiah. In the Old Testament, hundreds of years before his birth, Isaiah and Malachi prophesied the coming of John the Baptist.

"A voice of one calling: 'In the wilderness prepare the way for the LORD; make straight in the desert a highway for our God'" (Isaiah 40:3).

"'I will send my messenger, who will prepare the way before me. Then suddenly the Lord you are seeking will come to his temple; the messenger of the covenant, whom you desire, will come,' says the LORD Almighty" (Malachi 3:1).

What dying words of Jesus on the cross were prophesied a thousand years before His death on the cross?

Throughout His ministry, Jesus used scripture from the Old Testament. He used scriptures from Deuteronomy to defeat three temptations issued by Satan. On the cross, He cried out a scripture that is in Psalm 22. This psalm was written 1000 years before the crucifixion of Jesus. As Jesus was being crucified on the cross, He cried out these words, "My God, My God, why has thou forsaken me?" These words are seen as a prophesy of what would happen to Jesus on the cross.

✝ ✝ ✝ ✝ ✝ ✝ ✝ ✝

"My God, my God, why hast thou forsaken me?" (Psalm 22:1).

How many demons did Jesus cast out of Mary Magdalene?

As Jesus continued His ministry from town to town, His disciples followed Him: the twelve and others. There were also women who followed Him during His ministry. One woman in particular was Mary Magdalene. Magdalene is not her sir name. The name represents the city where she was from: Magda. She was a woman with sin in her life. Jesus cast out seven demons from her and healed her.

✝ ✝ ✝ ✝ ✝ ✝ ✝ ✝

"And it came to pass afterward, that he went throughout every city and village, preaching and shewing the glad tidings of the kingdom of God: and the twelve were with him, And certain women, which had been healed of evil spirits and infirmities, Mary called Magdalene, out of whom went seven devils" (Luke 8:1-2).

How many of Jesus' miracles are recorded in the book of John?

Throughout His three and a half years of ministry, Jesus performed many miracles. Each gospel records a different number of miracles. Matthew records 20 miracles, Mark records 20, Luke records 21, and John records 8. However, of the eight miracles recorded in John, six are not mentioned in the other three gospels.

The eight miracles recorded in John are
1. Turns water into wine
2. An official's son is healed at Cana
3. A lame man is healed
4. Jesus heals a man born blind
5. Lazarus is raised from the dead
6. The second miraculous catch of fish
7. Five thousand people are fed
8. Jesus walked on water.

What are the seven sins God hates?

God put man on this earth to live a righteous life according to His commands. However, man rebelled against what God had set in place. There are many types of sins. There are seven sins that scripture points out that God hates: a proud look, a lying tongue, a hand that kills innocent people, a mind that thinks up wicked plans, feet that hurry off to do evil, a witness who tells one lie after another, and someone who stirs up trouble amongst others.

"There are six things the LORD hates, seven that are detestable to him: haughty eyes, a lying tongue, hands that shed innocent blood, a heart that devises wicked schemes, feet that are quick to rush into evil, a false witness who pours out lies and a person who stirs up conflict in the community" (Psalm 6:16-10).

Whose seat did Jesus say the Scribes and the Pharisees sat on?

The Scribes and the Pharisees were two groups that represented the Jewish community during Christ's days on Earth. These groups were leaders. One was an authority of the law, and the other was an authority of the written scripture. Jesus said they had a prideful attitude about their position. Thus, Jesus described them as hypocrites who sat in Moses' seat. They abused their authority by claiming themselves to be above others. They let their pride create in them a bad representation of the Word of God.

"Then spake Jesus to the multitude, and to his disciples, Saying The scribes and the Pharisees sit in Moses' seat: All therefore whatsoever they bid you observe, that observe and do; but do not ye after their works: for they say, and do not" (Matthew 23:1-3).

Who told Zacharias (John the Baptist's father) that his wife would conceive?

Angels in the Bible played an active role in people's lives just as they do today. They spoke to many people, believers and nonbelievers. One case is when an angel appeared to Zacharias, a priest, and told him he and his wife would have a son and to name him John.

✝ ✝ ✝ ✝ ✝ ✝ ✝ ✝

"Then an angel of the Lord appeared to him, standing at the right side of the altar of incense. When Zechariah saw him, he was startled and was gripped with fear. But the angel said to him: 'Do not be afraid, Zechariah; your prayer has been heard. Your wife Elizabeth will bear you a son, and you are to call him John'" (Luke 1:11-13).

Who prophesied that Jesus would be born in Bethlehem?

There are many prophesies about Jesus' birth, His return, and His ministry. One of the prophesies that stands out is the location where He would be born. The prophet Micah made this prophesy. He said Jesus would be born in Bethlehem.

"But thou, Bethlehem Ephratah, though thou be little among the thousands of Judah, yet out of thee shall he come forth unto me that is to be ruler in Israel; whose goings forth have been from of old, from everlasting" (Micah 5:2).

What did Jesus say He would leave to all after He left this earth?

Jesus was well aware of the things to come as He ministered to the people. He knew His time was short on this earth, and He was very concerned about the apostles and His other followers. They had grown to depend on Him, and He knew they were not quite ready to take on the divine task at hand. He, therefore, told them He would leave them a helper to help them in their ministry and the godly life they were to live. This helper is the Holy Spirit sent from God.

"But the Comforter, which is the Holy Ghost, whom the Father will send in my name, he shall teach you all things, and bring all things to your remembrance, whatsoever I have said unto you" (John 14:16).

What two elements did the Bible say Jesus came to us by?

The two elements the Bible says Jesus came to us by were water and blood. The water occurred when Jesus was baptized and God said, "This is my beloved son," and a dove descended upon Him. Then, when Jesus was on the cross, He shed His blood that we might be saved. At that same time, God gave witness to Jesus' identity by miracles of an earthquake, supernatural darkness, and the ripping of the veil of the temple. Through the water and the blood, Jesus' deity was validated by God.

"This is he that came by water and blood, even Jesus Christ; not by water only, but by water and blood. And it is the Spirit that beareth witness, because the Spirit is truth" (I John 5:6).

Who said Mary is blessed
among women?

When Mary, Jesus' mother, went to Judah to see Elizabeth, who was pregnant with John, she entered the house and greeted Elizabeth. When Elizabeth received the greeting from Mary, the baby leaped in her womb, and she was filled with the Holy Spirit. She then spoke aloud saying Mary is a blessing among women.

"And entered into the house of Zacharias, and saluted Elisabeth. And it came to pass, that, when Elisabeth heard the salutation of Mary, the babe leaped in her womb; and Elisabeth was filled with the Holy Ghost: And she spake out with a loud voice, and said, Blessed art thou among women, and blessed is the fruit of thy womb" (Luke 1:40-42).

What other name was the city of Bethlehem called?

Bethlehem is the city where Jesus was born. It is also called the "City of David" because it was David's birthplace. It was his home and the place where he was anointed by God via the prophet Samuel.

✝ ✝ ✝ ✝ ✝ ✝ ✝ ✝

"And Joseph also went up from Galilee, out of the city of Nazareth, into Judaea, unto the city of David, which is called Bethlehem; (because he was of the house and lineage of David" (Luke 2:4).

What were the two Mosaic ceremonies Jesus had to go through immediately after His birth?

One of the things the Jewish people did was recognize traditional ceremonies according to the laws. One was when a baby boy is born, he is to be circumcised when he is eight days old. The other ceremony was to take the baby when he is forty days old to the temple to be purified, a process of purification.

"And when eight days were accomplished for the circumcising of the child, his name was called JESUS, which was so named of the angel before he was conceived in the womb. And when the days of her purification according to the law of Moses were accomplished, they brought him to Jerusalem, to present him to the Lord" (Luke 2:21-22).

Who were the three persons angels appeared to concerning Jesus' birth?

There were prophets who prophesied the birth of Jesus. On the other hand, there were angels that appeared to several persons to address the birth of Jesus. They were Mary (the mother of Jesus), Joseph, and the shepherds.

✝ ✝ ✝ ✝ ✝ ✝ ✝ ✝

"Then Joseph being raised from sleep did as the angel of the Lord had bidden him, and took unto him his wife" (Matthew 1:24).

"And the angel came in unto her, and said, Hail, thou that art highly favoured, the Lord is with thee: blessed art thou among women" (Luke 1:28).

"And there were in the same country shepherds abiding in the field, keeping watch over their flock by night. And, lo, the angel of the Lord came upon them, and the glory of the Lord shone round about them: and they were sore afraid" (Luke 2:8-9).

What lie did Herod tell the wise men about what he wanted from Jesus?

Herod was the king of the Jews at that time. After hearing that the real king (Jesus) had come, he felt threatened and believed his position as the ruler of the Jews was seriously jeopardized. He then sought out to find baby Jesus and eliminate the threat by killing him. The wise men who came looking for Jesus to worship him met Herod in his quarters. Herod knew the wise men were on a mission to find him, so he lied and told them he wanted to find Jesus too, so he could worship him.

✝ ✝ ✝ ✝ ✝ ✝ ✝ ✝

"Then Herod, when he had privily called the wise men, enquired of them diligently what time the star appeared. And he sent them to Bethlehem, and said, Go and search diligently for the young child; and when ye have found him, bring me word again, that I may come and worship him also" (Matthew 2:7-8).

How many men did Moses select to go spy in the Promise Land and how were they selected?

As the Israelites came nearer to Canaan, Moses decided to send out spies and for them to report back, so they would know what they were going up against, though the Lord had already promised them victory. Moses selected twelve spies. The twelve represented each of the twelve tribes of Israel.

✝ ✝ ✝ ✝ ✝ ✝ ✝ ✝

"And the LORD spake unto Moses, saying, Send thou men, that they may search the land of Canaan, which I give unto the children of Israel: of every tribe of their fathers shall ye send a man, every one a ruler among them. And Moses by the commandment of the LORD sent them from the wilderness of Paran: all those men were heads of the children of Israel" (Numbers 13:1-2).

When Stephen was stoned, where did the stoner lay their coats before they stoned him to death?

Stephen was a one of the seven men chosen by the apostles to help them with various tasks in the church. Their appointed duties were to help free up some time for the apostles, so they could focus more on ministering to the people. Stephen was anointed not just to work but to preach the Gospel. When he began to preach, the unbelievers stoned him because he was preaching the kingdom of God is at hand and Jesus Christ is the Messiah. Before they stoned him, they lay their coats at the feet of Saul, better known as Paul.

✝ ✝ ✝ ✝ ✝ ✝ ✝ ✝

"And cast him out of the city, and stoned him: and the witnesses laid down their clothes at a young man's feet, whose name was Saul" (Acts 7:58).

Who saw "the heavens open"?

When the heavens open, that means God's presence is visible. There were two men that saw this and spoke those words. They were Jesus and Stephen.

"And it came to pass in those days, that Jesus came from Nazareth of Galilee, and was baptized of John in Jordan. And straightway coming up out of the water, he saw the heavens opened, and the Spirit like a dove descending upon him" (Mark 1:9-10).

"But he, being full of the Holy Ghost, looked up stedfastly into heaven, and saw the glory of God, and Jesus standing on the right hand of God, And said, Behold, I see the heavens opened, and the Son of man standing on the right hand of God" (Acts 7:55-56).

What healed the woman with the issue of blood and the blind man?

Healing is something Jesus did throughout His ministry. During several instances after Jesus had healed, He would tell the healed person what healed them. In the case of the woman with the issue of blood and the blind man, Jesus told them it was their faith that healed them.

✝ ✝ ✝ ✝ ✝ ✝ ✝ ✝

"But Jesus turned him about, and when he saw her, he said, Daughter, be of good comfort; thy faith hath made thee whole. And the woman was made whole from that hour" (Matthew 9:22).

"And Jesus said unto him, Go thy way; thy faith hath made thee whole. And immediately he received his sight, and followed Jesus in the way" (Mark 10:52).

What did Daniel not eat during his three-week fast?

Daniel was a strong believer in God who recognized and obeyed His commands. He refused certain foods that were forbidden by the Holy sacrament. He refused to eat the food the King commanded him to eat. And he fasted by not eating certain foods for three weeks. The foods he did not eat were bread, meat, and wine.

"In those days I Daniel was mourning three full weeks. I ate no pleasant bread, neither came flesh nor wine in my mouth, neither did I anoint myself at all, till three whole weeks were fulfilled" (Daniel 10:2-3).

The eighth plague consisted of a swarm of locusts. What brought the locusts over Egypt?

Moses took the message from God to Pharaoh in an effort to free His people. The king of Egypt would not listen to him and denied his request. This resulted in plagues that came over Egypt in the hope that it would persuade Pharaoh to let God's people go. The eighth plague consisted of locusts that came over Egypt. They were brought there by the East wind.

✝ ✝ ✝ ✝ ✝ ✝ ✝ ✝

"And Moses stretched forth his rod over the land of Egypt, and the LORD brought an east wind upon the land all that day, and all that night; and when it was morning, the east wind brought the locusts. And the locust went up over all the land of Egypt, and rested in all the coasts of Egypt: very grievous were they; before them there were no such locusts as they, neither after them shall be such" (Exodus 10:13-14).

How long did it take the Israelites to pass through the water of the Red Sea?

When the Israelites were finally free from Egypt, they proceeded to the Promise Land, which God had promised to them. Shortly after they left, Pharaoh had a change of mind and pursued them in an effort to bring them back. When they reached the Red Sea, Pharaoh's army was approaching them, and they had no other way of escape. God then created a dry pathway for them to cross the water by opening it up. It took the whole night for them to go through the sea.

✝ ✝ ✝ ✝ ✝ ✝ ✝ ✝

"And Moses stretched out his hand over the sea; and the LORD caused the sea to go back by a strong east wind all that night, and made the sea dry land, and the waters were divided" (Exodus 14:21).

"and the sea returned to his strength when the morning appeared" (Exodus 14:27).

Which prophet said, "I escaped by the skin of my teeth"?

When Job was going through his ordeals, he became very distraught. He began to think he had been alienated by his family, and his wife detested him. His friends had abandoned him. He felt the ones he loved had turned against him. Despite all this, he made it through. He described this overcoming experience as escaping by the skin of his teeth.

"All my inward friends abhorred me: and they whom I loved are turned against me. My bone cleaveth to my skin and to my flesh, and I am escaped with the skin of my teeth" (Job 19:19-20).

Who had an iron bed that was thirteen feet long and six feet wide?

The Israelites encountered many battles on their way to the Promise Land. When they were approaching the city of Bashan, the king of Bashan gathered his army and proceeded to attack them. With the help of the Lord, the king and army were defeated by the Israelites. When they entered their city, they found that the king of Bashan had a bed of iron thirteen feet long and six feet wide.

✝ ✝ ✝ ✝ ✝ ✝ ✝ ✝

"We took all the towns on the plateau, and all Gilead, and all Bashan as far as Salekah and Edrei, towns of Og's kingdom in Bashan. (Og king of Bashan was the last of the Rephaites. His bed was decorated with iron and was more than nine cubits long and four cubits wide. It is still in Rabbah of the Ammonites.)" (Deuteronomy 3:10-11).

Where did the term "scapegoat" come from?

In Old Testament times, when a person sinned, he/she had to make an atonement for his/her sin via an animal. One type of animal used was a goat. They would take two goats and cast lots. One would be chosen for the Lord, and the other one would be used to set loose in the wilderness as a scapegoat to atone for sin.

"He is to cast lots for the two goats- one lot for the LORD and the other for the scapegoat. Aaron shall bring the goat whose lot falls to the LORD and sacrifice it for a sin offering. But the goat chosen by lot as the scapegoat shall be presented alive before the LORD to be used for making atonement by sending it into the wilderness as a scapegoat" (Leviticus 16:8-10).

Where did the transfiguration take place?

The transfiguration of Jesus Christ was when Jesus took Peter, James, and John on a high mountain. On that mountain, Jesus' clothes became brighter than bright white. At that moment, there appeared Elijah and Moses. Then, there was the voice of God who said, "This is my beloved son." Thus, the transfiguration of Jesus displayed the Shekinah glory of God incarnate in the Son. The voice attested to the truth of Jesus' Sonship.

"After six days Jesus took Peter, James and John with him and led them up a high mountain, where they were all alone. There he was transfigured before them. His clothes became dazzling white, whiter than anyone in the world could bleach them. And there appeared before them Elijah and Moses, who were talking with Jesus. Peter said to Jesus, 'Rabbi, it is good for us to be here. Let us put up three shelters- one for you, one for Moses and one for Elijah.' (He did not know what to say, they were so frightened.) Then a cloud appeared and covered them, and a voice came from the cloud: 'This is my Son, whom I love. Listen to him!'" (Mark 9:2-7).

Which prophet wore a yoke around his neck?

Nebuchadnezzar, a Babylonian king, was preparing to attack Judah. They had a powerful army at hand, and if they would engage in battle with Judah and their allied nation, the Israelites would surely be defeated. God gave Jeramiah a message to take to King Zedekiah in Jerusalem. This message was demonstrative; he put a yoke around his neck to show the king they did not stand a chance of victory against the Babylonian army, and he called for the Israelites to surrender to them.

✝ ✝ ✝ ✝ ✝ ✝ ✝ ✝

"His is what the LORD said to me: 'Make a yoke, and fasten it on your neck with leather straps. Then send messages to the kings of Edom, Moab, Ammon, Tyre, and Sidon through their ambassadors who have come to see King Zedekiah in Jerusalem'" (Jeremiah 27:2-3).

Who used the phrase, "Shake off the dust of your feet"?

Jesus commissioned the twelve apostles to go out and announce the coming of the kingdom of God, just as John the Baptist had done. However, they were only to go to the Jews. They were to teach the Gospel to them and if they would not listen, they were not to get in any kind of debate or altercation with them. If that were the case, they were to shake off the dust from their feet, which means they were not to in any way compromise with them, but take the message to the next one.

"If it turns out to be a worthy home, let your blessing stand; if it is not, take back the blessing. If any household or town refuses to welcome you or listen to your message, shake its dust from your feet as you leave. I tell you the truth, the wicked cities of Sodom and Gomorrah will be better off than such a town on the judgment day" (Matthew 10:13-14).

Who can see evil in your heart?

When Jesus healed the paralyzed man on the mat, there were some men of the law who saw what took place. When Jesus healed the man, He told him to be encouraged and that his sin is forgiven. The men of the law began to think in their minds what Jesus did was blasphemy. Jesus knew what was in their heart and accosted them on this matter.

"But some of the teachers of religious law said to themselves, 'That's blasphemy! Does he think he's God?' Jesus knew what they were thinking, so he asked them, 'Why do you have such evil thoughts in your hearts? Is it easier to say 'Your sins are forgiven,' or 'Stand up and walk?' So I will prove to you that the Son of Man has the authority on earth to forgive sins'" (Matthew 9:3-6).

Which judge was nicknamed "Jerub-Baal"?

There were many pagan gods that the Israelites worshiped during certain periods of the Old Testament. One of them was the pagan god Baal. They built an altar to it. Gideon was a judge chosen by God to lead His people out of apostasy (turn away from God). Gideon took some of his servants and pulled down the pagan altar of Baal. The people afterward gave him the nickname "Jerub-Baal."

"From then on Gideon was called Jerub-baal, which means 'Let Baal defend himself,' because he broke down Baal's altar" (Judges 6:32).

Did Jesus have any brothers and sisters?

Jesus is the incarnate son of God. He was born of the virgin Mary who married Joseph. Jesus grew up to the age of thirty-three and a half before he was crucified. Through the marriage of Joseph and Mary, they had other children. Jesus had four brothers and at least two sisters.

"'Isn't this the carpenter? Isn't this Mary's son and the brother of James, Joseph, Judas and Simon? Aren't his sisters here with us?' And they took offense at him. Jesus said to them, 'A prophet is not without honor except in his own town, among his relatives and in his own home'" (Mark 6:3-4).

Who saw Jesus sitting on the right hand of God?

Stephen was one of the seven selected by the apostles to serve in the church in the role of a deacon to take away some of their workload. Stephen was full of love for the Lord and began preaching the Gospel of Christ. So many opposed what he was teaching, had him tried, and sentenced him to death by stoning. Just before he died, he said he saw Jesus sitting on the right hand of God.

"When the members of the Sanhedrin heard this, they were furious and gnashed their teeth at him. But Stephen, full of the Holy Spirit, looked up to heaven and saw the glory of God, and Jesus standing at the right hand of God. 'Look,' he said, 'I see heaven open and the Son of Man standing at the right hand of God'" (Acts 7:54-56).

Who built an altar and inscribed on it, "To an unknown god"?

When Paul arrived in Athens on his second missionary journey, he found the city full of idol worshipers. They had so many idol gods until they ran out of names for them. They made an idol of the unknown. They called it "to an unknown god."

"Paul then stood up in the meeting of the Areopagus and said: "People of Athens! I see that in every way you are very religious. For as I walked around and looked carefully at your objects of worship, I even found an altar with this inscription: TO AN UNKNOWN GOD. *So you are ignorant of the very thing you worship- and this is what I am going to proclaim to you"* (Acts 17:22-23).

Which prophet laid 390 days on his left side and 40 days on his right side?

Ezekiel saw the sins and how the Jewish people were not listening to what God was saying to them. Because of their sin, God allowed them to be captured by their enemy (the Babylonians). Ezekiel preached an action sermon by demonstration, so the people would better understand what he was preaching. In this sermon, preached through demonstration, he lay on his left side for 390 days and 40 days on his right side. That was a sign for the people of Israel to turn away from their sins.

✝ ✝ ✝ ✝ ✝ ✝ ✝ ✝

" "Then lie on your left side and put the sin of the people of Israel upon yourself. You are to bear their sin for the number of days you lie on your side. I have assigned you the same number of days as the years of their sin. So for 390 days you will bear the sin of the people of Israel.' 'After you have finished this, lie down again, this time on your right side, and bear the sin of the people of Judah. I have assigned you 40 days, a day for each year "' (Ezekiel 4:3-6).

What was the first bird mentioned by name in the Bible?

After about a hundred and fifty days, the water Noah's ark floated on began to recede. Noah, at a point, could not see any land. He had all types of animals onboard the ark, so he chose to fetch a raven from the pack and send it out in hope that land was nearby.

"The waters continued to recede until the tenth month, and on the first day of the tenth month the tops of the mountains became visible. After forty days Noah opened a window he had made in the ark and sent out a raven, and it kept flying back and forth until the water had dried up from the earth" (Genesis 8:5-7).

Who paid taxes with money from a fish's mouth?

Taxes have been around for a long time. During Jesus' visit to Earth, He recognized this custom of man. He, therefore, did not speak against it for the sake of not causing offense. Someone asked Peter if he should pay the temple tax, and Peter's response was yes. Jesus then came and was asked about tax. He told them to throw out the fishing line and the first fish you catch, take out the money (four drachma) from the fish's mouth and pay the taxes for Him and for them.

"When Peter came into the house, Jesus was the first to speak. 'What do you think, Simon?' he asked. 'From whom do the kings of the earth collect duty and taxes-from their own children or from others?' 'From others,' Peter answered. 'Then the children are exempt,' Jesus said to him. 'But so that we may not cause offense, go to the lake and throw out your line. Take the first fish you catch; open its mouth and you will find a four-drachma coin. Take it and give it to them for my tax and yours'" (Matthew 17:25-27).

How Well Do You Know the Holy Bible?

List of Commonly Committed Sins
and their Causes
*Bible verses used from ESV, NIV, KJV, and Topical Bible.

◆

abandonment	Psalm 34:18
abduction	Deuteronomy 24:7
abhorring judgment	Leviticus 26:43-44
abomination	Leviticus 20:13
abortion	Exodus 20:21-25
abusiveness	2 Peter 1:4
abhorrence of holy things	Act 2:33
accusation	Jude 1:9
adulterous lust	Matthew 5:27-28
adultery	Proverb 6:24-29
afflicting others	Isaiah 58:1-14
aggravation	Genesis 2:24
agitation	Proverb 12:25
aiding and abetting sin	**Colossians 3:12-17**
alcoholism	Galatians 5:21
all unrighteousness	1 John 1:9
anger	James 1:20
animosity	Ephesians 4:32
anxiety	Peter 5:6-7
apprehension	Thessalonians 1:1-12
argumentativeness	Timothy 2:15
arrogance	1Samuel 2:3
assaults	2 Samuel 13:1-39
astrology	Deuteronomy 28:9-12
atheism	Psalm 14:1
avariciousness	1 Timothy 6:9

Baal worship	2 Kings 17:16
backbiting	Proverbs 16:28
backsliding	Corinthians 13:5
bad attitude	Psalm 104:19
bad language	Ephesians 4:29
bearing false witness	Proverbs 19:5
big talk	Hebrews 10:25
being a workaholic	Proverbs 23:4
being quick to speak	Proverbs 17:28
belittling	Isaiah 55:8-9;
bereavement	Thessalonians 4:13
betraying Jesus	Matthew 27:3
bickering	Philippians 2:14
bigotry	Galatians 3:28 1
bitterness	Ephesians 4:31-32
black magic	Deuteronomy 18:9-14
blackmail	1 Corinthians 6:9-11
blasphemy	Matthew 12:31-32
boastfulness	Matthew 6:1-2
boisterousness	Exodus 23:1
bow to images	1 Timothy 2:5
bragging	Matthew 6:1-34
brainwashing	Philippians 4:8
break His commands	John 14:23-24
break his covenants	Luke 22:30
breaking covenants w/others	Hebrews 13:4
bribery	Exodus 23:8
brutality	Matthew 10:17-18
burn incense to gods	Leviticus 10:1-2
calamity `	Isaiah 45:7 Job 2:10
carelessness	Timothy 2:15
cars/riches of world	Matthew 6:24

carnality	1 Corinthians 3:3
casting God away	1 John 4:1
cause disagreements	Colossians 2:1-23
causing distress	2 Thessalonians 2:1-7
causing division	Romans 16:17-18
causing fear	John 14:27
causing men to err	John 10:1-42
causing offense	Corinthians 8:1-13
causing poor to fail	Luke 14:12-14
changing truth to lies	John 8:44
chanting of charms	Deuteronomy 18:9-12
cheating	James 4:17
come against His anointed	1 Samuel 24:6
complaining	Philippians 2:14
complacency	Proverb 1:23
conceit	Romans 12:16
concupiscence	Colossians 3:5
condemnation	Roman 8:1
condemning the just	Ephesians 4:32
causing conflict	Ephesians 4:32
confrontation	Matthew 18:15-20
confusion	Timothy 2:7
conjuration	Timothy 4:1
conspiring against God	Roman 13:1-14
consulting wizards	Leviticus 19:31
contempt	Romans 14:1-23
contention	Proverbs 3:30
controlling	2 Peter 1:5-8
conniving	Proverb 6:16-19
compulsiveness	Corinthians 9:27
contentiousness	Corinthians 11:16
contesting and resisting God	1 Timothy 3:1-7

corruption	2 Peter 2:19
counterfeiting Chris. work	2 Corin. 11:13-15
covering sin	Roman 6:33
coveting	Exodus 20:17
covetousness	Timothy 6:6-11
cravenness	Proverbs 23:31
criticalness	Colossians 3:12-14
crookedness	Proverb 11:3
cruelty	Proverb 12:10
using crystals	Acts 8:9-13
cursing God	Matthew 10:32-33
cursing	Ephesians 4:29
dealing treacherously	Romans 7:3
deceit	Proverbs 20:17
deception	Galatians 6:7-8
defamation	Titus 3:1-2
defeatism	Ephesians 6:10-18
defiantness	Genesis 3:1-24
defiling	Leviticus 15:31
degrading	Romans 1:24
dejection	Proverb 29:23
demon consciousness	Acts 16:16-18
demon worship	Ephesians 6:10-13
deny Jesus, resurrection	Matthew 10:33
dependencies	1 Thessalonians 4:12
depravity	Romans 1:29
desecration	Ezekiel 7:22
desires of this world	Colossians 3:5
despair	Isaiah 19:9
despising God	Samuel 2:30
despitefulness	Leviticus 20:13
despondency	Galatians 6:9

deviousness	Proverb 2:16
disagreements	Ephes. 4:31-5:2
disbelief	Mark 9:24
discord	Proverb 6:16-19
discrediting	2 Peter 1:21
discouragement	Exodus 6:9
disdain	Proverb 23:22
disgust	Ezekiel 23:17
dishonesty	Colossians 3:9-10
disobedience	Deuteronomy 28:15
disorderly	2 Thessalonians 3:6
disputing	1 Timothy 2:8
disrespectfulness	Corinthians 15:33
disruptive	1 John 2:15
dissension	Proverb 6:14
distantness	Deuteronomy 30:4
distrust	2 Timothy 3:16
division	1 Corinthians 1:10-13
divorce	Deuteronomy 24:1
domineering	Galatians 3:28
double-talking	1 Peter 5:8
double mindedness	James 1:6-8
doubt	Proverbs 3:5-8
dread	Deuteronomy 7:21
drug abuse	1 Corinthians 6:19
drunkenness	Proverbs 20:1
duplicity	Proverbs 6:16-19
drinking blood	Genesis 9:30
eating blood	Deuteronomy 12:33
eating unclean food	Acts 10:14
effeminate behavior	Deuteronomy 6:9
egotism	Philippians 2:1-10

enlarged imaginations	2 Corinthians 10:5
enter unrighteous agreements	Hosea 10:4
envy	Job 5:2
escaping	1 Corinthians 10:13
evil hearts & imaginations	2 Thessalonians 3:2
exasperation	Ephesians 4:1-3
extortion	Leviticus 6:4
failure in duty	Genesis 38:8
failure to glorify God	Psalm 69:12, 86:12
falsehood	Job 21:34
fantasizing	James 1:14-15
fault finding	John 7:24
fear	2 Timothy 1:7
fear of disapproval	2 Kings 8:19
fear of man	Proverb 29:25
fetishes	Romans 7:8
fighting	Proverb 28:25
flattery	Proverbs 29:5
foolishness	Corinthians 1:18
folly	Job 42:8; Psalm 69:5
forcefulness	Matthew 11:12
fornication	1 Corinthians 7:2
fortune telling	Leviticus 19:3
fraud	Luke 16:10-13
fretting	1 Peter 5:5-7
frustrations	2 Samuel 13:2
fury	Job 40:11
giving offense	Genesis 20:16
gloominess	Zephaniah 1:15
gluttony	Proverbs 23:2
gossip	Proverbs 11:13, 20:19
greed	Matthew 23:25

grieving	Nehemiah 8:10, 8:11
grumbling	Exodus 16:7
guilt	Hosea 13:16
harlotry	Nahum 3:4
harshness	Malachi 3:13
hating God	Exodus 20:5
hating	Titus 3:3; Jude 1:23
haughtiness	Jeremiah 48:29
high-minded	1 Corinthians 1:19
homosexuality	1 Corinthians 6:9
hopeless	Isaiah 57:10
horoscopes	Leviticus 19:31
human sacrifice	Deuteronomy 18:20
hypocrisy	Matthew 23:28
idleness	2 Thessalonians 3:6
idle words, deeds, & actions	Matthew 12:36-37
idolatries	Jeremiah 14:14
ill will	Deuteronomy 15:9
inhumanity	1 John 3:15
imaginations	2 Corinthians 10:5
immorality	Jeremiah 3:9; Jude 1:4
impatience	James 5:7-8
impetuousness	Habakkuk 1:6
imprudence	Proverbs 14:8, 14:15
impurity	Leviticus 15:19
inadequacy	2 Corinthians 12:9
incest	Leviticus 18:6-18
incitement	Proverbs 29:11
indifferences	Revelation 3:15-16
inflating	Matthew 7:1
inflexibility	Philippians 4:1-23
inhospitality	Ezekiel 16:49-50

iniquity in your heart	Psalm 25:11;,51:9
injustice	Micah 6:8
insolence	Titus 3:2
intemperance	Proverbs 23:29-35
intentional sins	Hebrews 10:26
intimidation	Nehemiah 6:13-14
intolerances	2 Samuel 12:7
intellectualism, sophisticated	1 Timothy 6:20
inventing sin	James 1:4; Acts 2:28
inventing evil	Romans 1:24-32
inward wickedness	Ephesians 6:12
irrationality	Roman 1:20
irreverence	Nehemiah 5:15
jealousy	Exodus 34:14
being judgmental	Luke 6:37
justifying the wicked	Proverbs 11:1
kidnapping	Deuteronomy 24:7
killing	1 Samuel 19:5
lack of self-control	1 Corinthians 7:9
lawlessness	1 John 3:4; James 4:17
lasciviousness	Proverbs 2:16-18
laziness	Proverbs 12:24
lesbianism	Romans 1:27-27
levitation	Isaiah 60:1, 60:8
lewdness	Ephesians 5:5
lying	Proverbs 12:22
loathing	Psalm 119:158
longing for sin	1 Peter 2:1-25
loneliness	Psalm 25:16
loose morals	James 1:12
looting	1 Samuel 23:1
loving evil	Psalm 52:3

loving money	Matthew 6:24
loving praise	Philippians 2:3-4
lust	Matthew 5:28
lust of the eye	Matthew 5:28
lust of the flesh	1 John 2:16
lust of the mind	Psalm 25:11
lying to the Holy Spirit	Acts 5:1-5
lying with pleasure & delight	Colossians 3:9-10
madness	John 10:20
magic	Acts 8:9-13
making war	Micah 3:5
maliciousness	Exodus 23:1
manipulation	Galatians 2:4
manslaughter	Matthew 5:21
marauding	Joshua 8:27
masturbation	James 1:14-15
materialism	Luke 12:15
mischief	Ephesians 4:1-3
misery	Exodus 3:7
misleading	Matthew 18:6-7
mulishness	Leviticus 26:19
mocking	Proverbs 17:5
murder	Exodus 20:13
murmuring	Philippians 2:14
muttering	Isaiah 8:19
necromancy	Leviticus 19:31
negativism	Matthew 7:1-2
nicotine addiction	1 Corinthians 6:19
not being watchful	Matthew 24:24
occultism	Isaiah 8:18
obsessing	2 Corinthians 10:4-5
obstinacy	1 John 3:2

oppression	Deuteronomy 26:7
overbearing	Titus 1:7
pedophilia	Leviticus 18:23
persecuting believers	2 Timothy 3:12
persecuting, persecution	Acts 9:11
perversion	Leviticus 18:23
perverting the gospel	Acts 20:20
petulance	Isaiah 40:32
planning without God	Proverbs 16:9
plotting	Ezekiel 11:2
plundering	Ezekiel 39:10
pompousness	1 Timothy 4:13
pornography	Psalm 101:3
possessiveness	Mark 12:27
pouting	Proverbs 14:17; 15:18
prayerlessness	1 Thessalonians 5:17
prejudice	Galatians 3:28
presumption	2 Peter 3:1-18
pretend to be a prophet	2 Peter 2:1-22
pretension	2 Corinthians 10:5
pridefulness	Proverbs 11:2
pride of life	1 John 2:16
procrastination	1 Peter 5:7
profane God	Colossians 3:8
profanity unto God	1 Timothy 6:10
professing to be wise	James 1:1-27
prophecy by Baal	Deuteronomy 18:15
prophesying lies	1 John 4:1
propagating lies	Exodus 5:9
proudness	James 4:6
provoking God	Deuteronomy 4:25
provoking	Galatians 5:26

puffing up	1 Samuel 17:28
quarreling	Genesis 13:8
quenching the Holy Spirit	Solomon 8:7
questioning God's Word	Isaiah 55:8-9
raiding	Proverbs 24:15
railing	Proverb 102.8
raging	Psalm 37:8
raping	Deut. 22:25-28
rationalization	Luke 14:18-20
ravaging	1 Chronicles 21:12
rebellion	Psalm 106:43
rebuking	2 Timothy 3:16
recklessness	Numbers 22:32
refusing to hear	Matthew 11:15
refusing to repent	Jeremiah 15:19
refusing to be humble	1 Chronicles 7:14
refusing to live in peace	Roman 5:1
rejecting reproof, salvation	Proverbs 5:12, 6:23
rejecting God and His Word	Luke 9:23
rejection	Romans 11:15
rejoicing in others' adversity	Colossians 2:18
rejoicing in idols	1 Corinthians 10:14
rejoicing in iniquity	John 14:1-31
repetitiveness	Hebrews 10:26
reproaching good men	Job 27:6
resentment	Judges 8:3
restlessness	Genesis 4:12
retaliation	Matthew 5:39
reveling	1 Samuel 30:16
reviling	Matthew 5:11, 15:4
revenge	Leviticus 19:18
rigidity	Mark 9:18

robbing God	Malachi 3:8
robbery	Philippians 2:6
rudeness	Matthew 5:22
sadism	Nahum 3:19
scheming	Ester 9:25
scornfulness	1 Samuel 2:29
seduction	Acts 18:13
seeking self-gain	Matthew 6:33
seek pleasures from world	Matthew 6:33
self-accusations	1 Corinthians 3:16-17
self-admiration	1 Corinthians 3:16-17
self-centeredness	Matthew 16:24
self-condemnation	1 Peter 3:3-4
self-corruption	Luke 16:15
self-criticalness	Proverbs 12:18
self-deception	2 Peter 3:9
self-delusion	Titus 1:11-12
self-destruction	Matthew 7:13-14
self-exultation	Isaiah 45:25
self-glorification	Psalm 34:3
self-hatred	Ephesians 5:29
self-importance	Galatians 2:6
self-rejection	Psalm 34:17-20
selfishness	Philippians 2:4
self-pity	1 Thessalonians 5:18
self-righteousness	Luke 18:9-14
self-seeking	Romans 2:8
serving other gods	Joshua 24:15
sewing discord	Proverbs 6:16-19
sexual idolatry	Matthew 5:28
sexual immorality	Thessalonians 4:2-8
sexual impurity	Thessalonians 4:3-5

sexual perversion	Leviticus 18:23
oral sex	1 Corinthians 7:3-4
sodomy	Leviticus 20:13
shame	Isaiah 61:7
silliness	Proverbs 8:5
sinful mirth	Job 20:5
skepticism	Matthew 21:21
slander	Leviticus 19:16
slaying	Psalm 34:21
slothfulness	Proverbs 6:6, 19:15
snobbishness	Romans 12:16
soothsaying	Leviticus 20:6
sorcery	Leviticus 19:31
sowing seeds of hatred	James 4:11; 6:14
speaking curses	Isaiah 8:10
speaking incantations	Ezekiel 13:20
speaking folly	Job 42:8; Psalm 38:5
speculation	Matthew 12:37
spell-casting	Matthew 10:28
spiritual laziness	Proverbs 19:16
spitefulness	1 Peter 2:1-25
stealing	Ephesians 4:28
stiff-necked	Exodus 32:9
strife	Proverbs 20:3
striving over leadership	Colossians 3:23-24
struggling	1 Corinthians 10:13
stubbornness	Psalm 81:11-12
stupidity	Romans 1:22
suicidal thoughts	James 4:7
suspicion	Hebrews 11:6
swearing	James 5:12
take advantage of others	Luke 6:31

taking a bribe	Exodus 23:8
taking offense	Samuel 25:28
take God's Name in vain	Matthew 12:23
taking rights from poor	Ezekiel 18:16,18
teaching false doctrines	1 Timothy 1:3, 6:3
temper	1 Samuel 20:7
temptation	Matthew 6:13, 26:14
tempting God	James 1:13
theft	Matthew 15:19
timidity	2 Timothy 1:7
trickery, two-facedness	Genesis 3:1
trustless	Numbers 20:12
trusting lies	Psalm 118:8
trust own righteousness	John 14:1
trusting wickedness	John 12:36
tumults	Amos 2:2
turn your back on God	Matthew 10:33
unbelief	Mark 9:24
unbridled lust	Thessalonians 4:4
uncleanness	Matthew 12:43
uncompromising	James 4:17
undermining	Job 15:4
unequal yoked no-believers	2 Corinthians 6:14
unfairness	Matthew 20:13
unfaithfulness	Leviticus 6:2
unforgiveness	Mark 11:25
unfriendliness	Proverbs 18:1
ungratefulness	Luke 6:35
unholy alliances	1 Kings 3:1
unholy habits	Timothy 5:13
unmanly	Genesis 1:26
unmercifulness	Matthew 18:21

unrepentant	1 John 1:9; Rev. 2:5
unrighteousness	Jeremiah 22:13
unruliness of tongues	Micah 6:13
usury	Nehemiah 5:10, 5:7
unthankful	Colossians 3:15, 4:2
untruthfulness	Proverbs 12:17, 14:5
Unworthiness	Luke 17:10
using tarot cards	Leviticus 20:6
vain imaginations	Zachariah 10:2
vanity	1 Samuel 16:7
vengeance	Romans 12:19
viciousness	Matthew 26:52-54
violence	Job 16:17; Oba. 1:10
vulgarity	Ephesians 4:29, 5:4
white magic	Leviticus 19:31
wickedness	Timothy 5:8
willful sin	Hebrews 10:26
willful, intentional sin	Numbers 3:1-51
winking with evil intent	Job 15:12; Prov. 3:29
witchcraft, withdrawal	Deuter. 18:9-12,18:20
withholding a pledge	Proverb 3:27, 23:13
without concern	Timothy 6:20
without natural affection	John 13:34-35
without mercy	Luke 6:36
working for praise	Galatians 5:16-26
worldliness	1 John 2:15-17
worrying	Matthew 6:25-34
worshipping possessions	Revelation 9:20
worshipping our works	Roman 1:25
worshipping the creation	Roman 1:25
worshipping of planets	John 4:23
wrathfulness	Psalm 37:8

wrong doing	Exodus 23:2
zealous make others sinful	Romans 10:2
zealousness in outward show	Philippians 1:27

References

Bible Gateway. Biblegateway.com. January 2019

Zondervan. (2003). NIV Quest Study Bible, Revised, Rapid, Michigan 49530.

The Holy Bible. (1998). KJV Holman Bible Publishers, Nashville, Tennessee.

Amplified Translation. Biblegateway.org

King James Translation. Biblegateway.org

New King James Version.

New Living Translation. Biblehub.com

KJV Holman Study Bible. (2012). Holman Bible publisher. Nashville, Tennessee.

About the Author

Elder Rayford Jones Elliott is a minister of the gospel of Jesus Christ. He is a devout follower of Christ Jesus because he loves the Lord with his whole heart. As a minister, he teaches and preaches the Word with great fervency in an attempt to save the lost by bringing them into the knowledge of the truth. In his local church, where he has been a member for eighteen years, Elder Elliott serves as the president of the Men's Fellowship and adult Sunday school teacher. He conducts weekly discussion groups, thereby demonstrating his dedication to spiritual development of men. It is his desire to instill in them the same love and zeal for Christ Jesus he possesses.